POLY A DISASTER

A STORY ABOUT SACRIFICING REASON FOR LOVE

ANISE TOWNSEND

GOD'S STAR ANISE LLC

❀ Formatted with Vellum

To the women who came before me.

My grandmother, who embodied strength long before anyone called it resilience. A woman who endured years of physical abuse yet still found ways to love, nurture, and survive. Your endurance built the foundation beneath generations of women who came after you.

To my mother, the oldest of six girls, who carried responsibilities far heavier than she should have at such a young age. A woman taught that provision was love and survival was more important than softness. I now understand the emotional weight you carried while trying to hold everyone else together.

And to my aunts, who helped raise me when my mother could not always be present. Thank you for the wisdom, protection, humor, honesty, and love you poured into me throughout my life. So much of who I am was shaped by the lessons each of you unknowingly planted inside me.

This book is for all of you.

For the women who endured when they deserved to thrive.

For the women who survived long enough for me to finally choose healing.

Your strength lives inside every page.

AUTHOR'S NOTE

This book is not an attempt to villainize the people I loved.

It is not a book condemning polyamory, marriage, divorce, sexuality, or even heartbreak itself. Nor is it a story about one person destroying another. Human relationships are rarely that simple.

This memoir is an honest reflection of what happens when unresolved wounds, emotional neglect, longing, trauma, love, desire, fear, and self-abandonment collide all at once.

For a long time, I believed survival and suffering were evidence of love. I believed endurance was noble. I believed sacrificing pieces of myself to preserve relationships made me loyal, strong, and worthy.

I now understand differently.

The pages ahead contain uncomfortable truths—not only about the people I loved, but about myself. There are moments in this story where I was hurt deeply. There are also moments where I hurt others, ignored my own boundaries, accepted less than I deserved, and confused emotional intensity with intimacy.

This book is not written from the perspective of a woman who believes she was perfect.

It is written from the perspective of a woman who finally became honest.

Honest about the relationships that shaped her.

Honest about the childhood wounds that influenced her choices.

Honest about the ways emotional starvation can make even unhealthy love feel intoxicating.

And most importantly, honest about the healing that became possible once she stopped abandoning herself to keep everyone else comfortable.

Names, identifying details, and certain timelines may have been altered for privacy purposes. However, the emotional truth of this story remains intact.

If you see pieces of yourself somewhere inside these pages, I hope you leave this book understanding one thing:

Love should never require the destruction of yourself to sustain it.

— Anise Townsend

CONTENTS

BEGINNING OF THE END

Sunrises over Kingsland were majestic.

Rays of light burst through endless rows of trees before settling softly against the suburban horizon. Kingsland was the kind of town people moved to when they were ready to slow down. A sleepy retirement haven where life moved quietly and nobody seemed to be in a rush.

But I wasn't there to rest.

I was there to escape.

Escape the chaos I had created.

Chaos disguised as love.

What I thought was love.

What I prayed was love.

What I convinced myself was love because the alternative meant admitting I had spent years emotionally starving inside relationships that looked successful from the outside.

The sunrise felt symbolic then.

A new beginning.

A fresh start.

But looking back now, I understand Kingsland was never my beginning.

It was my awakening.

I just didn't know it yet.

When I married Lee, the very thought of him wanting another woman terrified me. Marriage, to me, was supposed to be the ultimate security blanket. He was my forever and I was supposed to be his.

Completely.

Exclusively.

Whole.

While most children dreamed of becoming doctors, lawyers, entertainers, or athletes, I dreamed of being someone's wife. I fantasized about marriage the way little girls in movies fantasized about castles. I wanted partnership. Devotion. The kind of love songs promised existed.

I loved love.

Or at least the version of love I had created in my head.

Naive.

Romanticized.

Unrealistic.

But deeply sincere.

Looking back now, I understand my childhood played a tremendous role in shaping that longing. Growing up emotionally hungry, I mistook being chosen for being loved.

And I desperately wanted to be chosen.

My mother was the oldest of six girls. Most of them eventually married, but only one stayed married. The lessons the women around me passed down about men were rooted more in endurance than intimacy.

"Niggas ain't shit."

"The best way to get over one man is to get under a new one."

Love was never described as safe or emotionally nourishing. Men were temporary. Necessary, maybe. Useful, even.

But never fully trustworthy.

No one taught me that love should feel emotionally safe.

No one taught me softness.

No one taught me relationships could nourish me instead of simply exhausting me.

So when I met a man who worked hard, paid bills consistently, protected his family, and came home every night, I thought I had beaten the odds.

Lee and I built what many people would have called a beautiful life. We had a blended family of three boys and one girl, a comfortable home, stable careers, and over a decade of marriage behind us. At a time when so many marriages around us seemed to dissolve overnight, especially in African American communities where healthy examples of long-term love were scarce, we wore our years together like a badge of honor.

And honestly, we had earned them.

Marriage was not easy for either of us.

We were two stubborn people dragging barrels full of childhood wounds, survival tactics, pride, and emotional baggage into the same house while trying to convince ourselves it looked like love.

But it was our marriage.

And for a long time, survival felt close enough to happiness that I stopped questioning the difference.

Lee was nearing the end of over twenty years of military service. Kingsland was supposed to be our final stop before civilian life. A transition. A reward after decades of sacrifice and structure.

To the outside world we looked like we had made it.

But what people could not see was how emotionally exhausted I had become.

The loneliness inside my marriage had started years before everything unraveled.

Long before other people entered the picture.

Long before blurred boundaries, emotional confusion, and choices neither of us were truly prepared for.

Long before my marriage officially began collapsing, parts of me had already started disappearing quietly.

Lee was a provider in every sense of the word.

The mortgage was paid.

The lights stayed on.

The children were protected.

He went to work every day and carried the weight of responsibility on his back like it was second nature.

And for a long time, I convinced myself that should have been enough.

After all, compared to the stories the women in my family carried, my marriage looked successful.

I was not being physically abused.

I was not struggling financially.

I was not raising children alone.

That became my measuring stick.

Not happiness.

Not intimacy.

Not emotional fulfillment.

Just survival with fewer bruises.

But emotional intimacy between us always felt slightly out of reach.

Like trying to touch someone standing behind glass.

Physically, Lee was present.

Emotionally, he always seemed somewhere far away.

At first, I thought maybe I simply needed to love him harder.

Serve him better.

Be softer.

More patient.

More understanding.

So I tried earning love through acts of service.

I cooked.

Cleaned.

Supported his dreams.

Managed the household.

Handled emotional labor quietly while hoping every completed task might somehow unlock tenderness in return.

A vulnerable conversation.

A kiss that lingered.

Affection without obligation.

Something that made me feel emotionally chosen instead of merely functionally necessary.

But most days ended the same way.

With me still hungry.

Still waiting.

Still hoping.

There were nights I lay beside him feeling lonelier married than I had ever felt alone.

That realization filled me with shame because I believed grateful women were not supposed to feel empty inside stable marriages.

So instead of confronting my loneliness honestly, I learned to minimize it.

Rationalize it.

Swallow it quietly.

Because pain had been attached to love for most of my life, I never stopped to question whether emotional neglect was still a form of suffering.

Instead, I adapted.

I became performative.

I shrank my needs until I could barely hear them myself.

That silence became normal.

Routine became normal.

Loneliness became normal.

Until Kingsland.

Until the sunrise.

Until I finally made choices that forced me to confront myself honestly.

Until the life I spent years trying to preserve finally revealed a truth I had spent most of my adulthood avoiding:

I had spent most of my life mistaking survival for love.

And the road where my marriage ended would eventually become the place where my healing began

THREE DAY LEE

Lee and I were both in the military when we met.

At the time, we had mutual friends on social media but had never actually crossed paths in real life. One day he sent me a friend request. I reluctantly accepted it, but almost immediately messaged him asking:

"Do I know you?"

He replied claiming he thought we had been stationed together before.

A clever lie.

He knew very well he did not know me, something he later admitted.

At the time though, I remember laughing when he apologized and jokingly said:

"I'm not stalking you."

"Yes you are," I replied.

And honestly?

He kind of was.

For several days afterward, he messaged me constantly trying to convince me to go out with him. But I kept resisting because I was preparing for a seven-month deployment in less than two months and saw no point in emotionally entertaining someone knowing I would be leaving soon.

In my mind, temporary relationships already came with expiration dates attached to them.

I did not want another almost-love.

Another unfinished connection.

Another person to miss.

But Lee was relentless.

Not disrespectfully.

Just persistently hopeful.

Eventually he said:

"The worst thing that could happen is you get a free meal."

Something about that line disarmed me enough to finally say yes.

Looking back now, agreeing to that date changed the entire trajectory of my life.

Because our first date did not last a few hours.

It lasted three days.

Once we finally met in person, neither of us wanted to leave the other's presence. The connection between us was immediate. Intense in a way that felt almost unsettling because of how quickly we opened up to one another emotionally.

We talked about everything.

Poetry.

Childhood wounds.

Past relationships.

Heartbreak.

Loneliness.

The deep longing we both carried to finally feel fully loved by someone.

We had both experienced relationships where love felt uneven. Relationships where we gave more emotionally than we received. Relationships where being chosen felt uncertain instead of secure.

I think we were both starving in ways we did not fully understand yet.

There was something intoxicating about finally meeting someone who seemed to understand the language of my loneliness fluently.

By the second day of our first date, we were already looking at rings.

Rings.

That sounds absolutely insane now saying it out loud.

But at the time, it did not feel crazy at all.

It felt certain.

Like I had finally stumbled into the safety I had been searching for my entire life.

That was the dangerous part.

The connection felt cosmic.

Not because we truly knew one another deeply yet.

But because I recognized myself inside his wounds.

And because I was emotionally hungry enough, recognition felt identical to destiny.

Not long into our relationship, Lee found out he received orders to Ohio.

At the time we were both stationed in Virginia, and suddenly our relationship faced a decision point much sooner than either of us expected.

My options felt simple on paper.

Either I reenlisted and stayed in Virginia...

or I got out of the military and followed him to Ohio.

But emotionally, the decision felt much bigger than geography.

Lee was adamant about one thing from the very beginning:

He was not doing a long-distance relationship.

He wanted me to come with him.

I remember telling him:

"Girlfriends don't follow boyfriends. Wives follow husbands."

And shortly afterward, we got married.

At the time, marriage did not just feel romantic.

It felt like security.

Commitment.

Permanence.

Proof that I was finally being chosen completely.

So when I made the decision to leave the military and build a life with him, I was not simply choosing a relationship.

I was choosing an entirely different future.

One built around us.

We got married in a courthouse with two witnesses and two of our children present. Shortly afterward, Lee moved to Ohio with his two small children from a previous marriage while I stayed behind finishing the remainder of my military contract.

His mother came down from Detroit to help with the kids until I eventually joined them a few weeks later.

By the time I finally arrived in Ohio, we were still trying to settle into our new life together. Unpacking boxes. Buying household items. Learning how to exist together as a newly blended family.

One day, his mother and I went to Walmart shopping for things for the house.

I remember us casually strolling through the aisles picking up little things we needed when out of nowhere she looked at me and said:

"I don't think Lee really loves you. I think he needed somebody to help him raise his kids."

I felt devastated instantly.

Not angry.

Not defensive.

Just…heartbroken.

Why would you tell me this now?

What exactly was I supposed to do with that information?

I did not cry in front of her, but I wanted to.

Honestly, part of me wanted to run away right then and there.

But where exactly was I supposed to go?

By then, I had already gotten out of the military to become a stay-at-home wife and mother to four small children. I had no money of my own. No nearby family to run to. No real safety net outside my marriage.

Lee was my plan A and B.

So instead of leaving a man who potentially only married me for childcare, I made a decision quietly inside myself.

If he did not truly love me yet…

perhaps I could earn his love.

Looking back now, that moment explains more about my marriage than I understood at the time.

Because from that point forward, I stopped simply being his wife emotionally.

I became a woman constantly trying to prove herself worthy of being fully loved.

Years later, I started referring to the man I met during those first three days as "Three Day Lee."

Because the version of him I fell in love with never fully appeared again.

At least not consistently.

The openness.

The vulnerability.

The emotional intimacy.

It vanished almost as quickly as it arrived.

And for the next thirteen years of marriage, part of me kept hoping Three Day Lee would come back.

I kept believing if I loved him hard enough, supported him deeply enough, sacrificed enough pieces of myself, eventually I would find my way back to the man who stayed awake talking to me for three straight days like love itself had finally found him too.

But looking back now, I realize I fell in love with who we both became during those first three days.

Two emotionally exhausted people desperate to finally feel chosen.

And sometimes the version of someone we fall in love with only exists briefly inside the beautiful illusion created when two lonely people finally feel seen.

EMOTIONAL DESERT

From the outside, my marriage was something to envy.

We had built a life together.

Children.

A home.

Responsibilities.

Years of shared history.

And for a long time, I convinced myself stability was the same thing as emotional fulfillment.

But it wasn't.

Somewhere along the way, our marriage slowly shifted from intimacy into functionality.

We became partners in survival.

Co-parents.

Providers.

Problem-solvers.

But emotionally, something between us had started drying out quietly.

Like land going years without rain.

At first, the changes were subtle enough to ignore.

Longer silences.

Less affection.

Conversations becoming transactional instead of intimate.

We talked about bills, schedules, responsibilities, work, the children—but very rarely about ourselves anymore.

Not deeply anyway.

Not vulnerably.

Sex eventually became a chore.

Not because I no longer loved my husband.

But because sex had quietly become the only time I received physical intimacy from him at all.

Outside of sex, affection felt scarce.

Transactional.

Almost inconvenient.

Lee was not naturally affectionate. He was not the kind of man who showered me with "I love you's," random kisses, soft touches, or emotional reassurance. In his mind, provision was love.

And for many years, I tried to convince myself that should be enough.

After all, that was how I had watched the women before me survive marriage.

Especially the women in my family.

You endured.

You adapted.

You stayed grateful for what was provided and learned not to ask for too much emotionally.

Softness was a luxury.

Survival was the priority.

So I learned to survive too.

Lee loved breakfast.

In many ways, it was his quiet reward for carrying our family.

Breakfast was part of his routine, and I viewed it as part of my responsibility to make sure he started his day properly. Before I started working full time myself, breakfast in bed was normal in our marriage.

Not appreciated.

Expected.

November 18, 2017 my sister called to tell me my mother had been admitted to the hospital once again. Initially we did not panic, she'd been sick for years so hospital stays were a regular occurrence.

But something about this time felt different.

Around one o'clock the morning of the 19th I was jolted out of my sleep by my phone ringing.

It was my sister and she was hysterical.

The hospital called, it was time to say goodbye.

My mother went into cardiac arrest numerous times before she was called. My mother had a DNR on file but for whatever reason the doctors were not aware. My sister told them my mother would not want this. She asked them to keep her alive long enough for her to get there so my mother would not leave this world alone.

By three a.m. my mother was gone.

Despite the complicated relationship we shared, despite the distance, despite the pain, she was still my mother.

And I was still her daughter.

I remember laying down briefly afterward, emotionally exhausted, only to wake up to Lee asking about breakfast.

"No days off," I replied.

He smiled.

I smiled too but I wasn't joking.

And strangely enough, I was not even angry that he asked.

I was angry that I obliged.

Less than twenty-four hours after losing my mother, I was standing in the kitchen performing normalcy because somewhere along the way I had learned my grief did not excuse me from caregiving.

That realization stayed with me for years.

Because it forced me to confront how deeply I had been conditioned to prioritize everyone else's comfort before my own humanity.

Eventually, I realized survival without tenderness still felt emotionally lonely no matter how stable my life appeared.

There were times I had to cry, argue, or create tension just to get something as simple as a kiss before he left for work in the morning.

Something so small.

So basic.

So human.

And yet I found myself begging for it like emotional scraps.

Looking back now, I realize how much that slowly impacted my self-worth over time.

Because when I constantly had to request, negotiate, or emotionally earn affection, eventually I stopped feeling desired naturally.

I started feeling tolerated.

And I discovered there was a specific kind of loneliness that came from laying beside someone every night while simultaneously feeling emotionally untouched by them.

There were nights I would lay awake scrolling endlessly on my phone while he slept beside me, wondering how two people could share a bed and still feel worlds apart.

I wanted to reach for him.

To be held.

To feel wanted without having to ask first.

But after enough rejection—intentional or not—I eventually stopped asking altogether.

That was how my emotional desert formed.

Not through one catastrophic moment.

But through accumulation.

A lack of watering.

A lack of softness.

A lack of emotional nourishment over time.

And the dangerous thing about emotional neglect is that it does not always look abusive from the outside.

Sometimes it looks responsible.

Stable.

Functional.

Sometimes the person hurting me was still showing up every day paying bills, going to work, helping raise children, and technically doing everything "right."

That complexity made it harder for me to fully acknowledge my unhappiness.

Because Lee was not a monster.

He was a provider.

A hard worker.

A man carrying his own emotional conditioning and understanding of love.

But eventually, I had to admit something to myself that felt almost shameful at the time:

I was starving inside my marriage.

And emotional starvation changed me.

Attention started feeling intoxicating.

Kindness felt seductive.

Affection felt addictive.

When I went long enough without emotional nourishment, even crumbs began to feel like a feast.

At the time, I did not fully understand how vulnerable that loneliness was making me.

I only knew I missed feeling connected.

Missed feeling soft.

Missed feeling seen.

And somewhere deep inside myself, a quiet ache had already begun forming long before I ever met another woman.

HE NEVER FUCKED

I was the one who introduced the idea of polyamory.

Not Lee.

At the time, I convinced myself it was my idea entirely. But looking back now, I understand the idea did not appear out of nowhere. It grew quietly inside the emotional loneliness already living inside my marriage.

By the time poly entered our relationship, emotional distance had already taken up permanent residence inside our home.

Lee had a wandering eye.

I knew it.

Even before I had proof, I felt it.

Women online.

Late-night conversations.

Emotional energy being invested everywhere except back into our marriage.

And every time I confronted him about it, his response remained painfully consistent:

"I never fucked them."

As if betrayal only counted when bodies touched.

As if emotional disloyalty somehow hurt less because clothes stayed on.

I begged him, tears streaming down my face, to stop.

Stop the inappropriate online conversations.

Stop the public thirsty comments.

Stop the random text messages from other women.

Not because I wanted control over him, but because I could feel our marriage slowly drifting emotionally. Every conversation he entertained with another woman felt like a reminder that parts of him were being poured elsewhere while I sat home pretending not to notice the distance growing between us.

But instead of reassuring me, he adapted differently.

He blocked me from his social media.

According to him, I could not be hurt by what I could not see.

That logic shattered something inside me.

Because it taught me very quickly that preserving his access to other women mattered more than preserving my emotional safety.

And still…

I stayed.

Emotional erosion does not happen all at once.

It happens slowly.

Quietly.

One rationalization at a time.

One compromise at a time.

One swallowed hurt at a time.

Until eventually I became so accustomed to emotional discomfort that dysfunction started feeling normal.

There were nights I pretended to be asleep while he laid beside me messaging other women in the dead of night.

The glow from his phone illuminated parts of his face

while I laid there silently watching him exchange messages with strangers with more emotional intent than he had given me in years.

Every so often he would glance over to make sure I was still "sleep."

As if betrayal somehow became less real if I did not openly witness it.

Physically, he was present.

Emotionally, he always seemed somewhere far away.

And over time, I realized distance was one of the ways he maintained control emotionally.

Lee knew I struggled with anxious attachment. He knew silence unsettled me deeply. Anytime conflict arose or I challenged something he did not like, he had a habit of emotionally disappearing. Sometimes he would not speak to me for days.

Other times, weeks.

The silence felt suffocating.

Not loud.

Not explosive.

Just cold absence where connection used to live.

And eventually, I learned how to survive it.

I learned to keep the peace.

To soften my tone.

To minimize my feelings before they became inconvenient.

I apologized even when I was not wrong because reconciliation mattered more to me than fairness.

I learned to swallow relational violations quietly because being emotionally ignored felt unbearable.

Another example of this showed up in something as simple as my hair.

Lee liked long hair.

Ironically, when we first met, my hair was short. But

shortly after our first date, he started sending me Bible scriptures about women cutting their hair. At the time, I interpreted it as preference. Maybe even protectiveness.

I did not recognize it as control yet.

The truth was, I preferred my hair short.

It made me feel more like myself.

Lighter.

More confident.

But one time I cut my hair without telling him beforehand.

When he saw it, he was furious.

Not screaming furious.

Worse.

Cold.

Distant.

Silent.

He did not speak to me for two days.

And that silence said everything.

I understood very quickly that certain choices about my own body no longer fully belonged to me without emotional consequences attached to them.

After that, I learned to ask first.

Not because I genuinely needed permission.

Because I knew what happened emotionally when I did not.

Conditioning like that becomes dangerous over time.

Not because someone physically forces you into obedience.

But because eventually peace starts feeling more valuable than autonomy.

So little by little, I stopped choosing myself simply to avoid being emotionally shut out again.

That dynamic shaped me in ways years of therapy would have to undo.

I could not remain emotionally honest for long inside a relationship where love often felt conditional upon my silence.

So little by little, I adapted.

Not because I was weak.

Because I was trying to preserve connection the only way I knew how.

And despite how lonely I became emotionally inside my marriage, one thing I took quiet pride in was the fact that I never laid with another man while I was with Lee.

Not once.

And it was not because opportunities did not exist.

Men approached me constantly over the years.

At work.

Online.

In public.

Sometimes respectfully.

Sometimes boldly.

But I always turned them down.

That mattered to me deeply because despite everything happening inside my marriage, I still saw myself as loyal to it.

Especially physically.

Part of what hurt so deeply later was hearing Lee call me every name imaginable during the collapse of our marriage.

Bitch.

Whore.

Disrespectful.

Disloyal.

Because in many ways, I had actually been the opposite.

For years, I remained fiercely loyal to him physically even while emotionally starving beside him.

But my loneliness was never about needing another man.

It was about needing connection.

Tenderness.

Affection.

To feel emotionally chosen and seen.

And somewhere along the way, I had started confusing emotional deprivation with normalcy simply because I had survived inside it for so long.

So when I finally confronted Lee about the emotional distance growing between us, he never admitted to what I already knew was happening.

Instead, he blamed my mental health.

Said my mind was playing tricks on me.

That I was imagining things.

Too sensitive.

Too emotional.

Too paranoid.

And after hearing those responses enough times, I slowly started distrusting my own instincts more than his behavior.

That was the dangerous thing about emotional manipulation.

It not only make me question him.

Eventually, it made me question myself.

Polyamory did not begin because I was sexually adventurous.

It began because I was emotionally starving.

I wanted connection.

Attention.

Novelty.

Validation.

I wanted to feel desired again.

Seen again.

Chosen again.

And somewhere inside my desperation to fix what felt broken between us, I convinced myself expanding our marriage emotionally might somehow save it.

I framed it as freedom.

As honesty.

As evolution.

But honestly?

Part of me was trying to outrun loneliness without fully confronting it.

Polyamory gave us permission to explore other people, but it never addressed the emotional fractures already existing between us.

If anything, it magnified them.

Because healthy relationships do not suddenly become healthier by adding more people into unresolved pain.

And underneath our marriage sat years of unmet emotional needs neither of us knew how to properly articulate.

I was lonely.

Deeply lonely.

But I had become so focused on surviving the relationship that I stopped recognizing my loneliness as something worthy of attention.

Instead, I adapted.

I performed understanding.

I convinced myself being "cool" and "accepting" made me evolved.

I normalized behaviors that quietly devastated me emotionally because I thought love meant endurance.

And honestly?

Part of me feared if I pushed too hard, I would lose him completely.

So instead of demanding emotional safety, I negotiated with my own discomfort.

That became the pattern.

Every time something hurt me emotionally, I learned to minimize myself instead of confront the pain directly.

That was how my self-abandonment began.

Not loudly.

Quietly.

Through repetition.

Through survival.

Through convincing myself that accepting less somehow made me easier to love.

And somewhere inside all of that compromise, the foundation of my marriage slowly began cracking beneath me long before I finally admitted it aloud.

LIAR LIAR

The first woman we introduced into our poly journey broke every rule we had established except being bisexual.

Her name was Amber.

At least that's what I'll call her in this book.

She was young.

Too young by our standards.

No children.

Wanted marriage one day.

And somehow, despite all the rules we had so carefully crafted, none of it seemed to matter once Lee saw her.

That should have been my first real warning that attraction rarely respects logic.

Lee initially told me he met Amber at a cigar shop while she was shopping for cigars for her father. The story sounded innocent enough at the time. Casual. Random. Organic.

But later, social media told a different story.

Amber and Lee had actually met while stationed on the same ship together in Virginia. He saw her crying in the hangar bay and escorted her back to his office to talk. According to him, she immediately responded to his kindness with flirtation and sexual advances.

He admitted he withheld the truth because he knew I would assume something inappropriate had already been happening behind my back.

And...

He was right.

That is exactly what I thought.

I believed he had been seeing her behind my back the entire time.

Emotional secrecy had already damaged trust between us long before poly officially entered the picture.

Still, I tried to move forward with an open mind.

Amber was beautiful.

Five-foot-nine.

Slim.

Dark-skinned with short blonde hair that framed her face perfectly. She carried herself with a confidence that filled the room before she even spoke. Her smile was infectious. The kind of smile that made people instinctively smile back.

But there was pain behind her eyes too.

At the time, I did not fully understand how much.

Amber had endured abuse in previous relationships and carried emotional wounds she tried disguising beneath humor, energy, and charisma. She had served in the military for several years, but underneath her vibrant personality was someone still deeply searching for stability, validation, and safety.

In many ways, I think I recognized parts of myself inside her.

We bonded over the devastating loss of our mothers.

We bonded over childhood trauma.

We bonded over our longing to be loved.

Lee's attraction to her was immediate and intense. But unlike the carefully imagined poly dynamic we had discussed for years, his connection with Amber felt driven more by desire than compatibility.

That became obvious quickly.

The week leading up to her arrival, we had the most passionate sex we'd experienced in years. We made love like we did when we first met. Desire that had long gone dormant between us suddenly felt reawakened by anticipation.

Like me, Amber was attracted to both men and women. Our first sexual encounter together felt surreal. Bodies tangled together in ways that almost felt cinematic. Music playing softly while moans, laughter, nervousness, and passion collided all at once.

For a moment, it felt exciting.

Free.

Like maybe we had finally unlocked the missing piece inside our marriage.

But outside of sex, very little about the arrangement actually made sense long term.

And despite my attempts to ignore it, something about the situation felt off from the very beginning.

The emptiness slowly began creeping back in.

Amber would come over late at night, spend time with us, laugh with us, sleep with Lee...

and then disappear before morning.

Every single time.

At first, the excuses sounded harmless.

She had anxieties.

Responsibilities.

Somewhere to be early.

But eventually the pattern became impossible to ignore.

She never stayed the night.

Not once.

I kept trying to warn Lee.

"There's something she's not telling us," I said repeatedly.

But lust has a way of silencing logic, especially when someone makes you feel desired.

The more I questioned Amber's behavior, the more defensive Lee became. To him, I sounded jealous or insecure.

To me, I sounded observant.

And when I finally confronted Amber directly with my concerns, the conversation escalated quickly. I was met with threats of violence inside my own home. The energy shifted almost instantly from playful to explosive.

Slowly, the entire house of cards began collapsing.

The lies eventually outnumbered whatever potential benefit existed in keeping her around.

Then the truth surfaced.

Although legal, she was years younger than she initially claimed.

Her mother was not deceased.

And Amber had a live-in boyfriend.

The same boyfriend she had been crying over in the hangar bay.

They had been together for years.

And suddenly everything made sense.

The disappearances.

The secrecy.

The emotional distance whenever conversations drifted beyond physical attraction.

She had never intended to integrate into our family structure because she already had a life outside of us.

And oddly enough, once the truth came out, I felt less angry than relieved.

Not because I enjoyed being right.

But because my intuition had not betrayed me.

For months I had ignored small internal alarms while trying to convince myself I was overthinking.

I had spent so much time minimizing my instincts inside my marriage that I almost no longer trusted them.

But this time, my instincts had been right all along.

Eventually, even Lee admitted the truth.

He confessed he had been thinking more with lust than practicality when it came to Amber. She was not a good fit for the kind of poly relationship we claimed we wanted.

She wanted her own man.

Her own family.

Her own future.

And honestly, she deserved that.

That realization forced us back to the drawing board.

Back to the rules.

Back to the illusion that we could somehow engineer love safely if we just chose more carefully the next time.

But looking back now, Amber represented something much bigger than our failed first attempt at polyamory.

She was the beginning of my awakening.

Because through her, I started noticing how often desire caused me to ignore truths standing directly in front of me.

I also began noticing how easily Lee could abandon me emotionally in pursuit of what he wanted physically.

And once I started seeing clearly, it became impossible to fully return to denial.

AMERICAN DREAM

After Amber, Lee and I convinced ourselves the problem had simply been compatibility.

She was too young.

Too emotionally unsettled.

Too disconnected from the structure we were trying to build.

So instead of questioning whether the entire idea itself was flawed, we returned to our original belief that the right woman simply had not appeared yet.

That's how I stayed inside a situation I probably should have left.

I convinced myself the issue was execution instead of foundation.

That's when Angela entered our lives.

Angela was the polar opposite of Amber.

More mature.

More nurturing.

More emotionally invested in the idea of building something long term instead of simply participating in excitement and experimentation.

She had no sexual interest in women, and at the time I convinced myself that was okay. We were still trying to figure out what would and would not work inside this lifestyle we were creating as we went along.

At first, she felt safer.

More stable.

Like maybe this was finally the version of polyamory we had been unsuccessfully trying to create all along.

And honestly, part of me desperately wanted it to work.

Because by then I needed proof that all the emotional compromising, discomfort, jealousy, confusion, and instability we had already experienced had not been for nothing.

I needed to believe we were evolving.

Growing.

Building something unconventional but beautiful.

Instead of slowly unraveling in real time.

Lee met Angela on an online dating site.

She lived in Brazil and wanted nothing more than to come to America and live the American dream.

We spent thousands relocating her and her child to America.

Because she only had a visitor's visa, a round-trip ticket was mandatory even though she had no intention of returning.

Fantasy quickly collided with reality.

I quickly learned it is easy to romanticize unconventional relationships when everyone still has space to leave and decompress separately.

It becomes much harder once emotional dynamics begin sharing kitchens, bathrooms, routines, responsibilities, moods, expectations, and silence.

That was the part I never heard anyone talk about openly.

Polyamory did not simply introduce additional love into our home.

It introduced additional emotional complexity.

And complexity magnified everything already unresolved.

At times, Angela felt deeply appreciative to be with us.

Other times, she felt emotionally restless.

There were moments she seemed grateful for stability and other moments where she appeared quietly resistant to it.

Living together exposed all the little emotional fractures none of us could avoid anymore.

Tension lingered in the smallest moments.

Body language.

Tone.

Silence.

Who someone sat next to.

Who received attention first.

Who withdrew emotionally when the atmosphere shifted.

I quickly realized there was no guidebook teaching people how to navigate emotional imbalance once multiple hearts began bleeding inside the same space.

And eventually, ours did.

One day, I found messages between Angela and another man.

Not innocent messages.

Intimate ones.

Flirtatious.

Secretive.

And buried inside those conversations was a line that hit me harder than anything else.

She told him she cried herself to sleep every night.

I remember staring at that message in disbelief because most nights she was sleeping peacefully beside my husband while I laid awake carrying the emotional weight of trying to hold everything together.

That realization hurt me in ways I still struggle to fully articulate.

Not because I believed she was evil.

But because it exposed how disconnected all of us had become from one another emotionally.

Everybody was lonely.

Everybody was searching.

Everybody was trying to feel chosen.

And none of us really knew how to communicate our unhappiness honestly before it spilled out sideways.

Still, the messages shattered something inside me immediately.

Not because we were poly.

But because trust was the only thing holding together an already emotionally fragile structure.

Without trust, everything collapsed.

We got into a heated argument.

I told her I did not trust her.

And I meant it.

Trust was essential in this type of dynamic because boundaries already existed in gray areas most traditional relationships never have to navigate. Communication had to be stronger. Transparency had to be stronger. Emotional honesty had to be stronger.

Otherwise everybody eventually started hurting each other.

At one point during the argument, I remember wanting to send her back to Brazil entirely.

That thought shocked me even as it crossed my mind because it forced me to confront something uncomfortable about myself too.

Control.

Fear.

Possessiveness.

The very emotions I once convinced myself polyamory would somehow eliminate.

But after the anger settled, something unexpected happened between Angela and me.

We talked candidly.

Really sincerely.

Not as two women sharing a romantic partner.

Not as rivals.

Just two women caught inside an emotionally complicated situation neither of us fully knew how to navigate anymore.

I finally asked her what she truly wanted.

Not what she thought we wanted her to want.

Not what fit into our arrangement.

Not what sounded good in theory.

But what genuinely made her happy.

And the truth was simple.

Angela did not want this life long term.

She wanted her own relationship.

Her own love story.

Her own partnership.

Her own forever.

And strangely enough, once the emotional smoke cleared, I understood that completely.

So instead of fighting her, I helped her.

I helped her create dating profiles.

Helped her navigate conversations online.

Helped her talk through what she actually deserved emotionally outside of our situation.

And eventually, she met Bobby.

The irony of it all was not lost on me.

After all the emotional chaos, confusion, jealousy, instability, and searching… Angela eventually found exactly what all of us had been looking for from the very beginning.

A relationship that belonged fully to her.

And eventually, she and Bobby got married.

She got her happily ever after.

And truthfully?

I was genuinely happy for her.

Because despite how messy our situation became, Angela was never truly the villain in my story.

None of us were.

We were simply emotionally wounded people trying to build permanence out of unresolved loneliness.

And underneath my anger sat a deeper truth I did not fully understand yet:

I was desperately searching for emotional security in situations built on emotional instability.

No amount of additional people, excitement, sex, or novelty could fix the loneliness already living inside me.

That loneliness belonged to something much older.

Something deeper.

Something I had spent most of my life trying to outrun through survival, relationships, performance, and distraction.

And by then, although I did not fully realize it yet, the emotional foundation beneath my marriage was already beginning to crack.

BBL WARRIOR

By the time Cynthia entered the picture, I was emotionally exhausted from trying to force incompatible people into a relationship structure none of us fully understood.

Amber wanted freedom.

Angela wanted stability.

I wanted accountability.

And somewhere in the middle of all that confusion, I started realizing something uncomfortable:

The women Lee chose were attracted to him and merely tolerating me.

That realization sat heavily on my spirit because it confirmed what I had quietly feared from the beginning.

This did not feel like expansion.

It felt like negotiation.

Or worse…

sanctioned cheating.

Cynthia—Cyn for short—was beautiful in the kind of way social media rewards aggressively.

She had the body everyone online praised.

The "mommy makeover."

The BBL.

The curated Instagram photos.

Luxury aesthetics funded far beyond her actual lifestyle.

She carried herself like an IG baddie long before that term became oversaturated online.

And immediately, I knew she did not align with the type of woman Lee constantly claimed he respected.

In fact, he despised the kind of woman she represented.

The irony was impossible to ignore.

Lee routinely criticized women who chose surgery over discipline. He often spoke negatively about attention-seeking behavior online and women who built their identities around male validation.

Yet here he was again...

drawn toward a woman who embodied everything he publicly claimed to dislike.

That was when I started understanding something deeper about attraction.

People are not always drawn toward what aligns with their values.

Sometimes they are drawn toward what feeds their ego.

And Cynthia absolutely fed his.

She was beautiful.

Attention-grabbing.

Sexual.

The type of woman other men openly stared at.

And I think part of Lee enjoyed feeling chosen by someone who looked like her.

But outside of physical attraction, very little about the dynamic felt emotionally promising.

Cynthia showed little interest in building a genuine relationship with me. Unlike Angela, who at least attempted integration into the household, Cyn seemed perfectly content maintaining a completely separate relationship with Lee while politely acknowledging my existence whenever necessary.

Her energy toward me felt tolerable, not warm.

And I noticed it immediately.

Our conversations were dry.

Surface-level.

Forced.

There was no emotional curiosity about me as a woman or partner. No desire to build friendship, intimacy, or connection outside of maintaining access to Lee.

At the time, I was still trying to convince myself poly could work if we simply found the "right" person.

But Cynthia forced me to confront a difficult truth.

Many people are comfortable sharing attention.

Very few are comfortable sharing emotional intimacy.

We arranged a weekend getaway for her to come to Georgia from Virginia. We planned to pay for everything and see whether the chemistry felt different in person than what already felt emotionally obvious over the phone. Her ticket was purchased and plans were already in motion.

A few days before her expected arrival, she and I had a private conversation that changed everything.

Unlike Lee, I had started asking uncomfortable questions early because I was no longer interested in temporary chemistry. I wanted to know whether someone's values actually aligned with the lifestyle they claimed they wanted. I also no longer wanted to waste time, money, or emotional energy on women searching for opportunity instead of genuine connection.

During our conversation, Cynthia mentioned attending Bible study regularly and trying to grow spiritually.

That immediately caught my attention.

So I asked her directly:

"Do you honestly believe your spiritual beliefs align with the kind of relationship you're saying you want?"

The silence that followed felt loud.

She paused for several seconds before quietly admitting:

"I don't know."

And strangely enough, I respected that answer more than anything else she said.

Because for the first time, someone stopped pretending certainty where confusion clearly existed.

Still, Lee wanted to move forward.

But one day before her flight, everything changed.

She called Lee and told him she no longer wanted to continue.

According to her, I did not like her.

And truthfully?

She was not entirely wrong.

Not because I hated her personally.

But because something about the situation felt fundamentally dishonest emotionally.

She did not want us.

She wanted him.

And there is a difference.

Lee exploded on me afterward.

He accused me of sabotaging the relationship from the very beginning because I never fully embraced Cynthia emotionally.

The argument escalated quickly.

Years of resentment spilled out all at once.

And finally, I said the thing I had been quietly feeling for months:

"This feels like sanctioned cheating."

Because from my perspective, these women were not emotionally investing in our marriage structure.

They were emotionally investing in him.

And I was simply the emotional obstacle they tolerated to access him.

Lee's response came fast and sharp.

"Then you pick."

At the time, he said it out of frustration.

But looking back now, that moment shifted something important inside me.

Because for the first time, the dynamic stopped revolving entirely around his desires.

And unknowingly, that single statement opened the door that would eventually lead me to Alex...

and ultimately back to myself.

TWIN

After Cynthia, something shifted between Lee and me.

Not necessarily for the better.

But definitely permanently.

For the first time since opening our marriage, I felt validated in what I had been trying to explain all along. The women Lee pursued were not truly pursuing us.

They were pursuing him while politely navigating around my existence.

And deep down, I think he knew it too.

That was why his frustration during our argument eventually turned into:

"Then you pick."

So I did.

Her name was Crystal.

And unlike the women before her, Crystal entered my life naturally.

Not through Lee.

Not through military circles.

Not through hidden flirtation disguised as friendship.

I met Crystal online through our shared love of beauty, fashion, femininity, and social media culture. We interacted casually at first, mostly through reposts and comments. I posted often about relationships, sexuality, and polyamory online, and she regularly engaged with my content.

Eventually, I told Lee to follow her page and see whether she followed him back.

She did.

And somehow, unlike the previous women, the entire interaction immediately felt lighter.

Easier.

Crystal was ambitious, intelligent, energetic, and emotionally engaging in ways I had not realized I was craving. She was tall like me, curvy like me, feminine like me. We jokingly called each other "twin" because we shared so many similarities in personality and interests.

And most importantly…

I genuinely liked her as a person.

Not just sexually.

Not just aesthetically.

I enjoyed talking to her.

That mattered more than I realized at the time.

There was only one real complication.

Distance.

We lived in Georgia.

Crystal lived in Philadelphia with her two sons, and unlike the fantasy scenarios Lee and I had once imagined, real-life responsibilities made relocation complicated.

Still, we wanted to explore the connection openly.

So we bought her a ticket to visit us for the weekend.

And from the moment she arrived, everything felt…easy.

There was no forced chemistry.

No emotional competition.

No awkward territorial energy.

We laughed naturally.

Talked endlessly.

Spent time together without the emotional heaviness that had followed previous situations.

Lee and Crystal got along immediately because they were both talkers. Meanwhile, Crystal and I connected emotionally in a way that felt refreshing after so much emotional confusion.

For the first time since entering poly, I experienced what emotional compatibility actually looked like.

And frankly?

That realization surprised me.

Because somewhere along the way, I had started associating struggle with passion.

Emotional confusion with chemistry.

Instability with excitement.

But Crystal felt peaceful.

Healthy, even.

There was just one problem.

I was not sexually attracted to her.

And that truth complicated everything.

Emotionally, she was probably the healthiest connection any of us had experienced up to that point. But physically, the spark I desperately wanted simply was not there for me.

And no matter how much I tried to convince myself emotional compatibility should have been enough, I could not force desire into existence simply because someone treated me well.

Eventually, the relationship faded naturally because of distance and circumstance.

No dramatic ending.

No betrayal.

No chaos.

Just life.

And oddly enough, that made the experience stand out even more.

Crystal remained in our lives long after the romantic aspect faded. She and Lee still spoke regularly, often venting to each other about life, relationships, stress, and parenting.

Meanwhile, my connection with Crystal taught me something important about myself.

I did not just want sex.

I did not just want attention.

I wanted emotional intimacy and desire.

Both.

And somewhere inside that realization, another truth quietly surfaced too.

Despite years of claiming I was only attracted to feminine women, something inside me had already begun shifting.

Because although I had dated several women by then, none of them had fully consumed my attention emotionally or physically the way my future encounter with Alex eventually would.

At the time, I did not know that yet.

I only knew one thing for certain:

For the first time in years, I had finally started paying attention to my own desires instead of centering everyone else's.

TOXIC CONNECTIONS

After Crystal, I started dating women on my own more openly.

Not because Lee and I had suddenly mastered polyamory.

We hadn't.

But somewhere between the failed dynamics, emotional confusion, and constant compromises, I had started reconnecting with parts of myself that had been buried beneath marriage and survival for years.

For the first time in a long time, my desires mattered too.

That realization felt intoxicating.

The first woman I dated independently was Lynette.

Unlike the previous situations, our relationship was built almost entirely on physical attraction and emotional escape. By then, I had developed a deep craving for feminine intimacy that had little to do with logic and everything to do with emotional starvation.

I wanted softness.

Attention.

Desire.

And initially, Lynette provided that.

She was married too, which strangely made the arrangement feel safer at first. There were already mutually understood boundaries. Neither of us was pretending we were building some grand future together.

At least that's what I told myself.

Because eventually, even casual arrangements develop emotional expectations when unhealed people become emotionally attached.

Lynette lived about an hour away, so most of our relationship existed through FaceTime calls, messages, and occasional visits. And almost immediately, I realized something important:

Physical chemistry alone could not compensate for emotional incompatibility.

Lynette had rules.

A lot of them.

The biggest being that she expected me to stop communicating with any woman I had previously been intimate with.

Under normal circumstances, maybe that request would not have sounded unreasonable. But in my case, most of the women in my social circle were women I had either dated, flirted with, kissed, or shared some level of chemistry with at some point.

My twenties had been wild in ways my marriage later buried beneath responsibility and routine.

Her request irritated me.

Not because I wanted to disrespect her boundaries, but because it felt controlling coming from someone still deeply entangled in her own toxic marriage while demanding emotional sacrifices from me she herself was not fully prepared to make.

That contradiction eventually became impossible for me to ignore.

Lynette constantly complained about her marriage, yet took no meaningful steps to leave it.

She wanted emotional rescue without personal accountability.

And eventually, the relationship became emotionally draining instead of exciting.

Toxic, even.

The kind of connection where conversations leave you feeling more exhausted than fulfilled.

Eventually we stopped speaking altogether.

But after several months, we reconnected and surprisingly developed a healthier friendship once the romantic expectations disappeared.

Looking back now, I realize many of the women I encountered during that season reflected different versions of emotional hunger back at me.

Some wanted escape.

Some wanted validation.

Some wanted saving.

Some simply wanted attention.

And truthfully, so did I.

I dated several other women after Lynette, but none of the connections lasted longer than a month or two. Some relationships fizzled because the chemistry was weak. Others collapsed because the emotional alignment was nonexistent.

No matter how beautiful someone was physically, eventually conversation mattered.

Consistency mattered.

Emotional safety mattered.

I was learning, slowly and painfully, that attraction alone could not sustain connection.

And yet…

desire still had power over me.

More power than I wanted to admit.

Because even while learning these lessons emotionally, I still had not encountered anyone capable of disrupting me completely.

Not until Alex.

At the time, I still believed I understood my type.

Feminine women.

Soft women.

Women who aesthetically mirrored pieces of myself.

I had never seriously considered masculine-presenting women attractive.

Or at least that's what I kept telling myself.

Until the day I drove into a small drive-thru restaurant in Kingsland looking for a chicken wrap…

and accidentally found the woman who would change my life forever.

CHICKEN WRAP

Last summer, I developed an almost ridiculous obsession with chicken wraps.

Not casually.

Obsessively.

I was Googling restaurants, driving across town, trying different places every few days searching for the perfect one. Looking back now, it feels symbolic somehow.

Like my spirit already knew I was hungry for something much deeper than food.

There was a small restaurant near me in Kingsland that I passed constantly but never paid much attention to. One evening, I decided to stop at Huey Magoo's on a whim and order a wrap.

Surprisingly...

It was perfect.

The sauce.

The greens.

The chicken.

Everything blended together so well I immediately became hooked.

So naturally, I went back.

And that's when I saw her.

Alex.

The moment I laid eyes on her, something inside me shifted.

She was beautiful in a way that completely disrupted everything I thought I knew about myself.

Masculine-presenting.

Androgynous.

Confident without trying.

She had beautiful curls and an energy that filled the room quietly instead of loudly. Nothing about her felt forced or performative. She simply existed comfortably inside herself in a way I found instantly magnetic.

I could not stop staring.

And apparently…

she noticed.

At the time, I was on the phone with my cousin in California, who also happened to be my best friend. The moment I saw Alex, I remember blurting out:

"I just met the most beautiful stud."

I said it jokingly at first, but even as the words left my mouth, I knew something about this interaction felt different.

Later, Alex told me she had immediately noticed me too.

After I left, she told her coworkers:

"I just met the most beautiful woman."

At first, she assumed I was simply passing through town off Interstate 95 like most travelers who stopped briefly in Kingsland before disappearing again.

But then she saw my Georgia license plate.

A local.

That changed everything.

My name was printed on the order ticket, and after I left,

curiosity got the best of her. She searched for me online and eventually found my TikTok page.

At the time, I had a decent social media following, so I never noticed when she initially followed me.

To me, she was still just the beautiful girl from the restaurant.

But to Alex, the search had already begun.

I returned to the restaurant several times afterward hoping to see her again.

And every single time...

she was not there.

After about a week or two, I finally drove in one evening and there she was.

The second our eyes met, we both smiled instantly.

The kind of involuntary smile you cannot fake even if you try.

I was grinning so hard my face hurt.

And she looked just as excited to see me.

That's when she casually said:

"You popped up on my For You page."

At first, I was flattered.

I remember thinking:

Damn, my TikTok really must be growing.

But something about the timing felt suspiciously convenient.

Sure enough, she eventually admitted the truth.

I had not randomly appeared on her page.

She searched for me intentionally using my name from the receipt.

And honestly?

That confession made the entire interaction even more attractive.

Because suddenly, I knew the energy between us had not been one-sided.

We laughed about it while standing there talking, and eventually I told her:

"Follow me and I'll follow you back."

Then I asked her how old she was.

"Twenty-five," she answered.

I immediately laughed and said:

"Oh hell, I'm going to jail."

She laughed too and replied,

"I'm grown."

The confidence behind the way she said it made something inside me nervous in the most exciting way possible.

Because right then, sitting outside Huey Magoo's, I realized something dangerous:

This was not harmless attraction anymore.

This felt like the beginning of something.

And deep down…

I think both of us knew it.

EMOTIONAL AWAKENING

After our second interaction at Huey Magoo's, I left smiling harder than I had in a long time.

There was something undeniably electric about Alex in person. The eye contact. The teasing. The confidence beneath her quietness. I could feel the chemistry every time we spoke face-to-face.

So later that evening, I messaged her on TikTok fully expecting the same energy to continue.

Instead...

the conversation was dry as hell.

Painfully dry.

Every question I asked got a short response with almost no effort to keep the conversation going. No curiosity. No flirtation. No engagement.

Nothing.

At first, I was genuinely confused.

Because the energy in person had felt so intense that I started questioning whether I imagined the entire thing.

Maybe she was just naturally charismatic.

Maybe I had mistaken excellent customer service for chemistry.

Maybe I had projected attraction onto someone simply because I wanted to feel desired.

Eventually, after forcing the conversation longer than my pride should have allowed, I stopped responding altogether.

I moved on.

Or at least I tried to.

Another week passed before I returned to the restaurant again.

And there she was.

The moment she saw me, she smiled immediately and said:

"I'm mad at you."

I laughed.

"For what?"

"You left me on read."

The accusation caught me so off guard I started laughing harder than she did.

"Girl, your conversation was dry as hell," I told her. "You didn't ask me not one question. It was like pulling teeth."

She burst into laughter trying to defend herself.

"Well maybe I'm shy."

"Maybe when I see a beautiful woman, I don't know what to say."

She kept talking while smiling nervously, and by then both of us were laughing so hard the tension between us shifted into something softer.

More natural.

More playful.

I had pulled through the drive-thru, so eventually she told me to wait while she helped another customer before coming back outside to continue talking to me.

And I actually sat there waiting.

Smiling like a love-struck teenager.

That alone should have told me how deep I was already falling.

When she returned, the energy between us felt completely different than before.

Comfortable.

Flirtatious.

Easy.

At some point, I ended up holding her phone in my hand, and without hesitation I called myself from it so she would have my number.

She was too busy admiring me to realize the transaction had taken place.

"We grown," she said. "We shouldn't even be talking through TikTok. I should already have your number."

I smiled and handed her phone back.

"My number already in there."

The confidence behind that move completely caught her off guard.

Her eyes widened before she started laughing again.

"Oh okay," she said. "You ain't playing no games."

I wasn't.

Not with her.

Because by then, something inside me had already recognized how rare the connection felt.

Once we started texting directly, everything changed.

The dry conversation disappeared completely.

Now we talked constantly.

Morning.

Afternoon.

Late into the night.

We joked, flirted, teased each other, and slowly began

learning one another beyond surface-level attraction. Every notification from her gave me a rush I was embarrassed to admit even to myself.

And for the first time in years, I felt emotionally pursued.

Desired.

Chosen back.

Around that same time, Lee and I had already planned a cabin trip to celebrate his retirement from the military. He was finally free to do things military life had restricted for decades—including smoking marijuana again for the first time in twenty-five years.

The trip was supposed to be about celebrating him.

And physically, I was there.

But emotionally?

My attention kept drifting back to Alex.

We texted nonstop the entire time I was away.

And somewhere during that trip, the first tiny red flags began appearing.

She became increasingly upset whenever I was not responding quickly enough.

If I became distracted for too long, her mood shifted noticeably.

At the time, I interpreted it as affection.

Interest.

Proof she really liked me.

Now I understand it differently.

But back then, emotional intensity still felt romantic to me because I had spent most of my life confusing emotional urgency with love.

I tried reassuring her repeatedly.

"We're here celebrating Lee," I explained. "I'll be home soon."

But even while trying to comfort her, I noticed something quietly shifting between us.

Her attachment to me was becoming emotional very quickly.

And truthfully?

So was mine.

THIS IS NOT THAT

Before things became serious between Alex and me, I had a conversation with her that I believed would protect us both.

It was the same conversation I had with every woman I dated outside of my marriage.

Not because I was trying to manipulate anyone.

Not because I was hiding my intentions.

But because honesty mattered deeply to me, especially in situations complicated enough to hurt people unintentionally.

By then, I had already seen what happened when emotions entered arrangements people were not fully prepared for.

So I spoke plainly.

Directly.

I told her:

"If you're looking for a situation where I'm going to leave my husband for you, this is not that."

"If you think I'm dating because something is missing and I'm trying to replace him, this is not that either."

"My husband is my best friend. I'm not going anywhere."

And at the time, I genuinely believed that.

Despite everything Lee and I struggled with emotionally...

Despite the loneliness.

Despite the wandering eye.

Despite the cracks spreading quietly through our marriage for years...

I still could not imagine my life without him.

That is important for me to acknowledge.

Because Alex did not enter my life through deception.

I warned her from the very beginning exactly where I stood emotionally.

I explained that I loved women too, but I was not searching for an escape plan or a replacement husband packaged inside a masculine-presenting woman.

This was not a situation where someone came in and stole me away from my life.

At least that was never my intention.

I wanted addition.

Expansion.

Connection.

Not destruction.

And after everything Lee and I had already survived together, I still believed poly could somehow coexist with marriage if everyone involved remained emotionally honest enough.

So I asked Alex directly:

"Are you sure this is something you can handle?"

Because I needed her to understand what she was stepping into emotionally before either of us got in too deep.

She looked at me calmly and said yes.

She said she respected my honesty because most people

would have lied about their marriage instead of speaking openly about its complexities.

She told me she understood the situation.

And if she ever reached a point emotionally where she could no longer handle it, she promised she would tell me.

At the time, that answer comforted me.

Because I wanted to believe maturity and honesty alone could prevent heartbreak.

But emotions do not care about agreements people make before attachment forms.

That was the part I did not fully understand yet.

I eventually learned people often agree intellectually to situations they are nowhere near emotionally prepared to survive.

I think all of us believed we were more emotionally evolved than we actually were.

That included me.

Because while I was warning Alex not to expect me to leave my marriage…

I was simultaneously becoming emotionally consumed by her in ways I had never experienced before.

After the cabin trip, I wasted no time getting back to her.

When we returned home, Crystal and Lee were upstairs in our bedroom hanging out while I rushed around the house trying to get myself together. My mind was completely occupied with Alex. Every part of me wanted to see her again immediately.

So instead of easing into the situation carefully…

I brought her to my house.

And the second Lee saw her, I knew there was a problem.

He instantly tensed.

Alex extended her hand politely, and while they shook hands, Lee silently sized her up from head to toe.

The tension between them was so thick it could have been cut with a knife.

I already knew why.

For years, I had insisted masculine-presenting women were not my type. I always claimed I liked feminine women exclusively, so seeing me emotionally drawn to a stud challenged something deeper inside him immediately.

This felt different to him.

More threatening.

More personal.

Rightfully so...

He was pissed.

But by then, I did not care nearly as much as I probably should have.

Somewhere deep inside me, I had already decided it was easier to ask forgiveness than permission.

Alex did not smoke or drink, so eventually we excused ourselves downstairs away from everyone else. What started as casual conversation stretched into hours.

We talked.

Laughed.

Shared stories.

At moments, we cried.

And sometimes we simply sat there staring at one another in silence like two people trying to understand why the connection between us felt so immediate.

Time disappeared around her.

At some point, I realized it was well after midnight and I still had work the next morning.

That's when my phone buzzed.

A text from Lee.

"Off tomorrow?"

"New position?"

Short.

Passive-aggressive.

Sharp enough to let me know he was absolutely not okay with what was unfolding downstairs.

I think that was the moment he realized this situation was fundamentally different from the women before her too.

Because eventually, he crept downstairs quietly like a Cheshire Cat trying to catch us doing…what exactly?

After all…

women weren't cheating.

WOMEN AREN'T CHEATING

Lee's reaction to Alex was immediate.

Not because of anything she said.

Not because of anything she did.

And certainly not because of any boundaries we had supposedly crossed.

It was her presence.

Her masculinity sat in the room like a challenge to everything he believed about himself. The moment they shook hands, I watched him size her up. His eyes moved across her frame with quiet hostility while his jaw tightened beneath forced politeness.

He disguised it as concern.

He disguised it as questions.

He disguised it as me "not knowing her long enough."

But that was a lie.

We never truly knew any of the women.

That had never mattered before.

Women had rotated in and out of our marriage under the convenient label of "poly." Some stayed a weekend. Some stayed longer. Some were flirtations online that eventually bled into reality. Some were simply distractions for Lee's wandering eye.

And despite how "mutual" everything appeared from the outside, there were times I did not even participate.

Sometimes I simply watched.

Other times, I would wake from my sleep to discover him already entangled with another woman beside me.

Those moments always left me emotionally disoriented.

Not because I lacked awareness of the arrangement.

But because emotionally, I was often trying to convince myself I was comfortable with situations my spirit had not fully agreed to yet.

Lee liked when I watched.

He liked the tension of it.

The competition.

The emotional intensity.

Looking back now, I think part of him enjoyed seeing women desire him simultaneously. There were moments where my jealousy almost seemed to validate him emotionally. As if my discomfort reassured him of his importance. My longing reassured him he was still wanted.

And because I was terrified of losing him, I kept trying to become the version of a woman who could endure it all gracefully.

I swallowed my discomfort so many times it became routine.

Every insecurity I voiced was minimized.

Every concern was reframed as me being emotional, jealous, difficult.

So eventually, I stopped expressing many of my feelings altogether.

Not because they disappeared.

Because I learned vulnerability often came back to me disguised as criticism instead of care.

Watching Lee be intimate with other women was heartbreaking.

Because the passion he displayed with them was the same passion I had been starving for inside my own marriage.

The version of Lee they received was not the same man I had been laying beside for over a decade.

With them, he seemed attentive.

Excited.

Engaged.

Playful.

Desired.

And I remember quietly wondering:

Where did that version of him go?

Because at home, I often felt emotionally invisible beside him.

One night, after watching him with another woman, I finally asked:

"Can I get what she got?"

An argument almost instantly followed.

But underneath the argument was a much deeper truth I struggled admitting aloud.

Part of me still hoped he would choose me completely.

That one day he would look at me and decide he no longer needed anyone else emotionally.

That we could return to being just us.

That I could finally stop competing for emotional intimacy inside my own marriage.

For years, I begged him in different ways to choose me emotionally.

Sometimes through tears.

Sometimes through silence.

Sometimes through overextending myself trying to become easier to love.

But everything changed once I met Alex.

Because for the first time in years, I experienced what it felt like to be chosen naturally instead of emotionally negotiating for scraps of affection.

And once I experienced that kind of emotional reciprocity, I could not unknow it.

I could not return to begging for the very thing someone else gave freely.

That was the real shift.

Not sexuality.

Not polyamory.

Not rebellion.

I had simply reached the point where surviving emotional starvation no longer felt acceptable once I finally remembered what emotional nourishment felt like.

But now suddenly there were rules.

Suddenly there was caution.

Suddenly there was morality.

Suddenly there was suspicion.

And the only difference was Alex.

Because Alex did not look feminine enough for him to dismiss.

She looked like competition.

We had returned from the cabin trip on the third. By the sixth, Lee was talking about leaving town and demanding a divorce. The shift was so abrupt it gave me emotional whiplash. One minute we were still pretending this unconventional arrangement was workable.

The next, my marriage was imploding because I brought home one masculine-presenting woman.

After all the women.

After all the compromises.

After all the humiliation I endured trying to be "understanding."

This was the straw that broke him?

Part of me could have calmed him down.

I knew that.

I could have reassured him.

Softened my tone.

Shrunk myself again to make him feel safer.

But I did not want to.

Because he had never done that for me.

When I cried over inappropriate conversations with women online, he blocked me from his social media instead of changing his behavior. His solution to my pain was concealment, not accountability. He taught me that my discomfort was inconvenient. So now that the discomfort belonged to him, I found myself emotionally detached from soothing it.

The text messages between us became more frantic by the hour.

At first, they almost sounded reasonable.

"She looks really young."

"She's twenty-five," I replied. "I saw her ID."

Then the questions became invasive.

"So where is she staying then?"

"She stays here and there."

"What in the world? Here and there is crazy."

"Times are hard out here."

Then came the judgment.

"So you met a homeless person. You didn't know she was homeless?"

But even then I defended her.

"Lee, she is good people and we need help with cooking and cleaning. Just get to know her."

Looking back now, I can hear myself trying to convince both him and me.

I wanted Alex to fit into the narrative somehow. I wanted her presence to make sense inside the crumbling architecture of my marriage. I wanted everyone to calm down long enough for me to figure out what I was feeling.

But emotions do not wait for logistics.

And attraction certainly does not wait for permission.

The more he questioned me, the more protective I became over her.

It was almost instinctual.

The texts moved from confusion to accusation so quickly it felt suffocating.

"When did you find everything out? I thought you just met her a week ago."

"Lee, why are you so upset?"

"I'm asking questions about who you said you met a week ago. You don't think this is weird?"

"Nope."

And I meant it.

Because what felt weird to me was his sudden outrage after years of emotional chaos I had been expected to normalize.

He became obsessive.

"Did the girl leave?"

"She went to work."

"Uber or someone picked her up?"

"I don't know if it was Uber or a coworker."

"Was she naked on the couch?"

The accusation was almost laughable.

"Nobody was naked on the couch. You just don't like her and you're going to look for any excuse."

Then came the paranoia.

"Same shit with Lynette and the other girl."

"I got cameras EVERYWHERE."

"You literally are changing the rules as you go," I texted back.

Because he was.

The rules had always bent in his favor until the moment I stopped bending with them.

The truth was, I barely even understood what was happening myself. Alex and I had spent hours downstairs talking while the rest of the house slept. Laughing. Crying. Sharing wounds like children comparing scars. Somewhere between midnight conversations and exhausted confessions, the air shifted between us.

I do not know when admiration became longing.

I only know I felt seen in a way that frightened me.

Making love to Alex awakened something inside me I did not realize had been dormant for years.

Just her presence ignited something in me emotionally.

With her, intimacy did not feel rushed.

It did not feel obligatory.

It did not feel performative.

We would spend hours wrapped inside one another's presence, talking, laughing, kissing, learning each other slowly. There was tenderness between us that felt almost disorienting after spending so many years emotionally starving inside my marriage.

She looked at me.

Really looked at me.

Not through me.

Not around me.

At me.

We would finish each other's sentences sometimes like our thoughts were moving alongside one another before either of us spoke them aloud. Being around her felt emotionally consuming in a way I had never experienced before.

And for the first time in my life, my body responded to intimacy in a way that completely overwhelmed me emotionally.

I cried afterward.

Not from sadness.

From the shock of realizing how disconnected from myself I had been for so many years.

I had never experienced pleasure that felt emotionally intertwined with vulnerability, safety, attention, and presence all at once. The experience left me disoriented in the most beautiful and terrifying way because suddenly I understood what had been missing inside me the entire time.

And once I experienced emotional and physical connection that made me feel fully alive, it became almost impossible to willingly return to emotional numbness.

That was the conflict slowly tearing me apart internally.

Part of me still clung to the familiarity of my marriage.

The history.

The family.

The life we had built.

But another part of me had finally awakened emotionally after years of surviving instead of truly living.

And I found myself torn between what felt familiar...

and what made me feel alive.

And Lee sensed it immediately.

Not because I confessed it.

But because men like him always notice when your attention no longer belongs to them.

At one point he texted:

"No need for sneaking and lying."

"Women aren't cheating remember?" I shot back.

That line cut deeper than either of us admitted.

Because for years, lesbian intimacy had only been acceptable when it entertained him or benefited him. But the moment emotional intimacy entered the room—real intimacy—everything changed.

Now suddenly it counted.

Now suddenly it threatened the marriage.

Now suddenly I was dangerous.

The irony was suffocating.

The same woman who had spent years minimizing herself to survive had somehow become the villain for finally feeling alive.

DEAR WIDDLE NICI

I always loved writing.

Long before therapy.

Long before marriage.

Long before I understood words could heal people besides myself.

I wrote because writing gave me somewhere to go emotionally when reality felt too heavy to survive inside directly.

To this day, I still have journals stacked away in storage filled with poems, thoughts, unfinished stories, prayers, heartbreak, anger, loneliness, and fragments of myself I did not yet know how to express out loud.

Writing became my first form of escape.

My first form of honesty.

My first safe place.

And years later, writing Dear Widdle Nici: Memoir of the Girl with the Beautiful Smile became no different.

While my marriage was collapsing around me in real time, I found myself escaping back into the little girl I had spent most of my life trying to outrun.

The little girl who felt unseen.

Unprotected.

Emotionally hungry.

The little girl who learned very early how to survive pain quietly.

A part of me genuinely believed that if I could finally heal her, maybe I would stop recreating relationships that required my suffering to sustain them.

So while everything around me felt chaotic emotionally, I locked in creatively.

I wrote obsessively.

Late at night.

After arguments.

Between tears.

Inside emotional confusion.

I poured myself into finishing something I had started years earlier because deep down, I needed to prove something to myself.

I needed to know I could complete something in the middle of chaos.

I needed to know I could stand on my own.

Finishing my first book became symbolic of something much larger than authorship.

For the first time in my life, I stopped abandoning myself halfway through my own healing.

Sentence by sentence.

Chapter by chapter.

I slowly started rescuing parts of myself I thought were gone forever.

The original plan was to release the book on my mother's birthday—October 3.

That date mattered deeply to me.

Despite our complicated relationship, my mother remained one of the most influential figures in my life.

Releasing the book during her birthday month felt symbolic. Like somehow I was honoring both the pain and the resilience passed down through generations of women in my family.

But life, grief, technology, and chaos had other plans.

Technical issues delayed the release, and I missed the date by five days.

At the time, I was devastated.

Five days felt enormous emotionally because I wanted the timing to be perfect.

I wanted the release to mean something sacred.

But looking back now, I realize the timing still mattered.

The book still arrived in October.

Still wrapped itself around my mother's memory.

Still became my homage to the woman whose wounds shaped so much of my understanding of love, survival, sacrifice, and pain.

And when the book finally released...

something unexpected happened.

People saw themselves inside it.

Women reached out to me crying.

Survivors.

Daughters.

Mothers.

People carrying childhood wounds they had buried for decades.

Some messages were long and detailed.

Others were only a sentence or two.

But many of them carried the same heartbreaking theme:

"I thought I was alone."

That sentence broke me every single time.

Because loneliness loses some of its power the moment somebody finally says:

"Me too."

For years, I thought my silence protected me.

But telling the truth connected me to people in ways silence never could.

Women shared stories of abuse.

Emotional neglect.

Self-hatred.

Abandonment.

Sexual trauma.

Depression.

And survival.

Some thanked me for finally putting language to emotions they had carried privately their entire lives.

Others simply thanked me for surviving long enough to tell the story at all.

And somewhere inside those conversations, I realized something important:

Healing myself publicly gave other people permission to confront their own wounds openly too.

That realization humbled me deeply.

Because suddenly the little girl who once wrote privately inside hidden journals had created something powerful enough to reach complete strangers emotionally.

For so long, I believed my voice only mattered in relation to other people.

As someone's wife.

Someone's daughter.

Someone's mother.

Someone's partner.

But writing that book forced me to finally see myself separately from the roles I spent my entire life performing.

I was a writer.

A storyteller.

A survivor.

A woman whose pain had purpose beyond destruction.

Dear Widdle Nici: Memoir of the Girl with the Beautiful Smile saved me.

Because while my marriage was falling apart externally, writing gave me somewhere safe to place my grief instead of drowning inside it.

I escaped the fall of my marriage by escaping to save the child inside me.

And somewhere between the pages, I finally began understanding something life had spent years trying to teach me:

Healing does not happen when I continue abandoning the wounded parts of myself.

Healing begins the moment I finally turn around and go back for them.

VILLAIN

The moment Lee realized my connection with Alex was emotionally real, everything changed.

Not gradually.

Immediately.

Because I had not been vocal publicly about the struggles inside my marriage, the collapse appeared sudden to people watching from the outside. To them, it looked like I woke up one day, met a woman, and destroyed my entire life impulsively.

Some people even whispered that I was going through a midlife crisis.

And truthfully, I understood why it looked that way.

What they could not see was the slow erosion that had already been happening quietly for years.

The loneliness.

The emotional distance.

The compromises.

The self-abandonment.

By the time Alex entered my life, parts of my marriage

had already been emotionally collapsing long before anyone else noticed the smoke.

But once Lee realized my connection with her was real, the rules that had governed our marriage for years suddenly no longer applied.

The same man who once dismissed my discomfort as jealousy now became consumed by suspicion, anger, and control. It was almost surreal watching someone who had spent years minimizing my insecurities suddenly unravel beneath his own.

Part of me enjoyed watching him unravel.

Not that I particularly enjoyed seeing him hurt, but he finally understood my hurt.

I had spent years swallowing pain quietly to preserve our marriage while he exercised freedoms he expected me to normalize.

Now suddenly I was dangerous.

Alex became an obsession for him almost overnight.

He stalked our social media.

Showed up places unexpectedly.

Sent endless messages.

Some angry.

Some manipulative.

Some almost desperate.

The emotional tone shifted constantly depending on whether he wanted control, sympathy, or intimidation.

And beneath all of it sat one undeniable truth:

He was terrified of losing me.

Not to another man.

To her.

I think that distinction mattered deeply to him.

Alex challenged more than just our marriage.

She challenged his masculinity.

His ego.

His understanding of his role in my life.

For years, women had existed inside our marriage only as long as they revolved around him emotionally. Even when I dated women independently, there was still an unspoken assumption that my marriage remained the emotional center of my life.

But Alex disrupted that balance immediately.

She loved me directly.

Openly.

Protectively.

And unlike the others, she did not seem interested in emotionally orbiting around Lee at all.

That terrified him.

The situation escalated quickly.

He began appearing anywhere he thought we might be.

Driving by.

Watching.

Texting obsessively.

At one point, he even went to Alex's mother's job and told her to tell her daughter to stay away from me.

By then, the situation had crossed far beyond jealousy.

It had become emotional warfare.

And still, somehow, I found myself emotionally split between fear and empathy.

Despite everything happening, part of me still understood his pain.

I knew betrayal lived inside him too.

Even if he could not articulate it properly.

Even if he weaponized it poorly.

Even if his behavior became cruel.

There were moments his messages shifted from anger into something uglier.

Gay slurs.

Obscenities.

Attempts to humiliate us both.

He mocked Alex's masculinity while simultaneously treating her like competition.

And eventually, the constant harassment became overwhelming enough that I blocked him entirely just to breathe.

That silence only escalated things further.

Meanwhile, Alex was terrified.

Not because she regretted loving me.

But because the situation around us had become emotionally volatile so quickly. She had entered my life expecting complexity, but not chaos on this scale.

Still...

instead of pushing us apart, the chaos bonded us even deeper.

We became emotionally inseparable during that season.

The more isolated we felt from everyone else, the more we leaned into each other for comfort. She became my emotional safe place while simultaneously existing at the center of the storm destroying my marriage.

That contradiction exhausted us both.

I loved her.

I truly did.

But loving her came attached to consequences I had not fully prepared myself to face.

At some point, the people around me quietly started treating me like the villain in the story.

The woman who destroyed her marriage.

The woman who chose another relationship over her family.

The woman who "changed."

Some people did not even bother hiding their conclusions.

Mutual friends started reaching out wanting "my side" of

the story, but I could already hear the judgment underneath their concern before the conversations even fully began.

Even Lee's ex-wife contacted me at one point.

I could tell many of them had already decided I was the problem before I ever opened my mouth.

But becoming the villain publicly was one thing.

Becoming the villain in my children's eyes nearly destroyed me.

For years, Lee and I had intentionally protected our boys from the specifics of our marriage. They never knew the details behind closed doors.

The arguments.

The emotional distance.

The loneliness.

The women.

The unraveling.

To them, Mommy and Daddy simply had "friends."

That was the extent of their understanding.

I wanted to keep it that way.

No matter how complicated things became between Lee and me, I never wanted our children carrying the emotional weight of adult problems they were too young to fully process.

But during one of his angrier moments, Lee outed everything to them.

And once he did, there was no taking it back.

In a fit of rage, he told them I was breaking up our family for "a homeless bitch with bed bugs."

Even writing those words now still hurts.

Not because of the insult itself.

But because that was the moment my children's perception of me shifted permanently.

Before Alex, our family still looked intact to them.

After Alex, she became the reason their home no longer felt safe or stable emotionally.

And children do not always understand emotional nuance.

They understand disruption.

Loss.

Change.

Suddenly, the woman they barely knew became attached to the collapse of everything familiar in their world.

So they hated her.

And honestly?

Part of me understood why.

Because from their perspective, everything changed the moment she arrived.

What they could not yet understand was that marriages often begin breaking long before children can visibly see the damage.

The collapse may look sudden to outsiders, but emotional erosion is usually slow, quiet, and years in the making.

Still, none of that softened the pain of feeling misunderstood by my own children.

That pain sat heavier than public judgment ever could.

Because strangers misunderstanding me was one thing.

But motherhood had always been the part of my identity I protected most fiercely.

And suddenly, even there, I became the villain too.

From the outside, I understood why the story looked simple.

People rarely see emotional erosion while it is happening slowly.

They only notice the collapse once everything finally falls apart publicly.

What nobody saw were the years leading up to it.

The loneliness.

The compromises.

The emotional neglect.

The self-abandonment.

People saw the explosion.

They did not see the slow leak that caused it.

And for a while, being misunderstood hurt almost as much as the divorce itself.

Because there is something deeply isolating about becoming the villain in other people's version of your story while privately fighting to survive your own.

And maybe from the outside, that version of events looked true.

But what people could not see was how long parts of me had already been emotionally dying before Alex ever entered my life.

She did not create the cracks in my marriage.

She exposed them.

That distinction mattered deeply to me, even if no one else understood it.

For years, I had survived by becoming smaller.

Quieter.

More accommodating.

More emotionally invisible.

And now suddenly, because I was finally choosing my own desires openly, I became difficult.

Selfish.

Dangerous.

A villain.

But sometimes people only call you selfish when your healing inconveniences the version of you that benefited them most.

BITCH

For months, I lived suspended between two lives.

One life was familiar.

Predictable.

Built over years of marriage, children, routines, sacrifices, and survival. It was the life I had spent over a decade protecting, even while pieces of me quietly disappeared inside it.

The other life felt uncertain.

Emotional.

Chaotic.

Terrifying.

But alive.

And somewhere between those two realities sat me—exhausted, confused, emotionally split down the middle trying to hold together things that no longer fit together naturally.

Alex wanted me to leave.

Not eventually.

Not someday.

Now.

From her perspective, the situation had already crossed

too many lines to repair. She watched Lee terrorize us emotionally, stalk us, insult us, and create tension everywhere we went. To her, reconciliation between Lee and me felt like betrayal after everything that had happened.

And honestly?

I understood why she felt that way.

But fear is complicated.

Especially when you have built your entire adult life around survival.

Leaving was not just emotional for me.

It was financial.

Practical.

Terrifying.

I was over one hundred thousand dollars in debt. We had children. A home. Shared responsibilities. Shared history. Shared survival. And despite everything happening, part of me still struggled to imagine life outside the structure of my marriage. A structure that had defined me for so long.

Alex saw freedom.

I saw uncertainty.

And uncertainty terrified me.

So even while knowing deep down that my marriage was deteriorating beyond repair, I kept hesitating.

Kept trying to smooth things over.

Kept emotionally splitting myself between the familiar pain I understood and the unknown future I did not.

Until the day something inside me finally snapped.

Lee and I were arguing again.

By then, tension had become the emotional soundtrack of our home. Every conversation felt sharp around the edges. Every interaction carried resentment beneath it. The house itself felt exhausted from absorbing so much anger and hurt.

Then during the argument, he called me a bitch in front of my sons.

And the room went silent.

Not loud silent.

The kind of silence that changes things permanently.

The kind that makes your spirit immediately recognize a line has been crossed that can never fully be uncrossed again.

In actuality,

I do not even know if my boys fully heard him.

I do not know if they remember it the way I do.

Maybe they missed it completely.

But I heard it.

I felt it.

And I could not let it go.

For years, I had made excuses for so much of his behavior.

The manipulation.

The silence.

The emotional neglect.

The wandering eye.

The humiliation.

I minimized things constantly trying to preserve my marriage and protect the image of the life we had built.

But this?

This felt inexcusable.

I remember looking at my boys and feeling something inside me shift instantly.

Disrespect behind closed doors was one thing.

I had already normalized too much of that.

But hearing their mother degraded openly in front of them shattered something much deeper inside me.

In that moment, my fear stopped mattering more than the example being set for my children.

I realized I could not spend years teaching my sons that this was what love looked like.

I could not teach them that women should tolerate emotional disrespect to preserve relationships.

I could not teach them that survival mattered more than self-respect.

And suddenly, staying no longer felt noble.

It felt dangerous.

Not physically.

Spiritually.

Emotionally.

Generationally.

That was the real breaking point.

Not Alex.

Not poly.

Not jealousy.

Not even the marriage itself.

The breaking point was realizing my children were learning love by watching us slowly destroy each other.

And I refused to pass that inheritance down to them.

For years, Lee had convinced me I could not survive without him.

That I would fail on my own.

That emotionally, financially, practically—I needed him more than I needed myself.

And for a long time, I believed him.

Fear sounds truthful when repeated long enough.

But standing there looking at my sons, something became crystal clear to me:

If I stayed, I would eventually lose myself completely.

And once a mother loses herself entirely, eventually everybody around her suffers from the emptiness that remains.

That realization terrified me more than divorce ever could.

So quietly, painfully, imperfectly…

I made my decision.

I was going to leave.

Not because I hated him.

Not because I stopped loving him overnight.

But because somewhere beneath the chaos, I finally understood something I wish I had learned much earlier in life:

Love should not require the slow destruction of myself to sustain it.

BEAUTIFUL DISASTER

Making the decision to leave felt powerful for exactly five minutes.

After that came terror.

Real terror.

Not the dramatic kind people post online attached to inspirational quotes and healing captions. I mean the kind of fear that sits in your chest at three o'clock in the morning while you stare at the ceiling wondering whether you just destroyed your entire life.

Once the adrenaline faded, reality arrived quickly.

I was over one hundred thousand dollars in debt.

I had children to think about.

Bills.

Responsibilities.

A life that had been financially and emotionally intertwined with another person for years.

And the hardest part was admitting much of that debt was tied to my own emotional emptiness.

Shopping became my coping mechanism long before I understood it was an addiction.

Every purchase gave me a temporary rush.

A temporary distraction.

A temporary feeling of fullness.

Clothes.

Shoes.

Beauty products.

Home décor.

Luxury items.

I kept buying things trying to recreate externally what I could not feel internally.

The more disconnected I felt emotionally, the more I consumed physically hoping something would fill the void.

But emptiness does not disappear simply because it is dressed beautifully.

In fact, the more I bought, the emptier I felt.

And eventually, I realized I was not shopping because I needed more things.

I was shopping because I needed comfort.

Validation.

Dopamine.

Escape.

Something to temporarily silence the emotional loneliness I had spent years trying not to acknowledge.

Lee often told people I was only with him because I was broke.

He did not mind saying it in front of anyone who would listen.

Friends.

Family.

Even Alex.

Sometimes it came out jokingly.

Other times it came out sharp enough to cut.

He would warn Alex constantly about my spending habits.

"She horrible with money."

"She'll have us in the poor house in no time."

At first, those comments embarrassed me deeply.

Not because they were entirely untrue financially.

But because they reduced something emotionally complicated down to irresponsibility.

The truth was, I was not horrible with money.

I was horrible with my emotions.

Shopping had become the way I coped with emptiness.

The way I soothed loneliness.

The way I rewarded myself for surviving.

But it was not just shopping.

I did a lot of things to numb pain instead of confronting it directly.

I stayed distracted.

Consumed.

Emotionally busy.

Because as long as I kept reaching for something outside of myself, I never had to sit still long enough to fully feel what was happening inside me.

And eventually, I realized avoidance was not healing.

I had to feel it to heal it.

Every purchase gave me temporary relief.

Temporary excitement.

Temporary comfort.

And for a few brief moments, buying things made me feel full emotionally in ways my relationships often did not.

But emotional voids do not stay filled long.

So I kept buying.

Kept consuming.

Kept trying to recreate internally through material things what I could not sustain emotionally inside myself.

Looking back now, I understand I was not addicted to things.

I was addicted to escape.

And honestly, realizing that forced me to confront myself differently.

Because once I stopped blaming my spending entirely on poor discipline, I finally had to acknowledge the pain underneath it.

The loneliness.

The anxiety.

The emotional starvation.

The constant need to soothe myself because I never fully learned how to sit peacefully inside my own emotions without reaching for something outside of myself first.

That realization forced me to confront another uncomfortable truth about myself:

Not all self-destruction looks dramatic.

Sometimes it arrives in packages at your front door.

And despite all the chaos surrounding my marriage, there was still grief.

That part surprised me the most.

People assume leaving unhealthy relationships feels freeing immediately.

Sometimes it does.

But sometimes it feels like mourning someone who is still alive.

I was grieving the marriage I thought I had.

Grieving the future I imagined.

Grieving the version of myself who believed love could survive anything if I just sacrificed enough pieces of myself to keep it alive.

For days, my emotions fluctuated constantly.

One moment I felt strong.

The next I felt guilty.

Then terrified.

Then relieved.

Then lonely.

Then determined again.

It was emotional free-fall.

And through all of it, I kept hearing Lee's voice in the back of my mind reminding me of all the reasons I supposedly could not make it on my own.

Fear has a way of replaying old conditioning like scripture.

But something unexpected happened during that season too.

People showed up for me.

Family.

Friends.

Co-workers.

Even people I had emotionally distanced myself from during my marriage quietly stepped forward reminding me I was not nearly as alone as I believed I was.

That realization hit me harder than expected.

Isolation had become so normal inside my marriage that I forgot community still existed outside of survival mode.

And strangely enough, while my personal life felt like it was collapsing publicly, another part of my life was expanding rapidly.

Dear Widdle Nici: Memoir of the Girl with the Beautiful Smile had entered the world.

My story.

My pain.

My truth.

For the first time in my life, people were not simply seeing me as someone's wife or someone's mother.

They were seeing me.

Anise.

Writer.

Survivor.

Woman.

That visibility scared me too.

Once people hear your truth, you lose the ability to hide comfortably behind performance.

The little girl inside me who spent years shrinking herself to keep love finally had a voice loud enough to reach other people.

And the response was overwhelming.

Women reached out sharing their own stories of abuse, neglect, abandonment, loneliness, survival, and healing. Some thanked me for saying things they had never found words for themselves.

Others simply said:

"I thought I was alone."

That sentence broke me every single time.

I understood exactly what they meant.

Loneliness feels heaviest when you believe nobody else can see it.

Meanwhile, my relationship with Alex remained emotionally intense but increasingly complicated beneath the surface.

The chaos that initially bonded us together had not disappeared simply because I decided to leave my marriage. If anything, reality began exposing just how emotionally exhausted both of us truly were.

Sometimes we loved each other beautifully.

Other times we triggered every wound inside one another.

And beneath all of it sat an uncomfortable truth I was slowly beginning to understand:

Freedom and healing are not the same thing.

Leaving my marriage freed me from one version of survival.

But freedom alone does not automatically heal the wounds that made survival feel familiar in the first place.

That truth unsettled me in ways I could not ignore.

For so long I believed changing my environment would automatically change my emotional patterns.

But wounds travel with you until you confront them directly.

Still…

despite the fear,

despite the grief,

despite the uncertainty,

despite the emotional wreckage everywhere around me—

I felt something I had not felt in a very long time.

Possibility.

Not certainty.

Not peace.

Not happiness.

Just possibility.

And after years of emotionally surviving instead of truly living…

that was enough to keep me moving forward.

EMOTIONALLY NAKED

Leaving my marriage did not magically quiet the chaos inside me.

If anything, the silence made certain emotions louder.

For years, my nervous system had adapted to emotional intensity.

Arguments.

Anxiety.

Tension.

Reassurance.

Conflict.

Long emotional conversations followed by temporary closeness.

Chaos had become so intertwined with love in my mind that peace initially felt unfamiliar.

Almost uncomfortable.

That realization frightened me more than I expected.

Because once survival mode slows down, you are finally forced to sit with yourself.

I was exhausted.

Emotionally.

Mentally.

Spiritually.

There were days I missed people who hurt me.

Days I missed Alex so intensely it physically ached.

Days I missed my marriage despite everything that happened inside it.

Not because I wanted the dysfunction back.

But because grief becomes complicated when your identity has been emotionally attached to people for so long.

Healing is not a straight line.

And trauma bonds do not disappear simply because logic tells you they should.

That was one of the hardest truths therapy forced me to confront.

And yes...

I returned to therapy.

I did not try navigating that season emotionally on my own.

That part matters to me deeply because I think people sometimes romanticize healing as though strength means isolating yourself and figuring everything out alone.

I knew better than that.

By then, I had already spent too many years emotionally surviving without properly unpacking the damage underneath my choices.

So I went back.

Not because I was weak.

I was finally honest enough to admit I needed help.

Therapy became one of the few places where I no longer had to perform strength constantly. I could unravel there. Cry there. Question myself there. Be angry there. Be confused there. Speak truths out loud that sounded terrifying inside my own head.

And slowly, I started recognizing patterns I had normalized most of my life.

I confused emotional intensity with intimacy.

I mistook being chosen for being loved.

I associated suffering with commitment.

And somewhere along the way, I learned to tolerate emotional inconsistency as long as occasional moments of affection followed afterward.

That realization humbled me deeply.

Healing required accountability too.

Not just accountability for the people who hurt me.

But accountability for the versions of myself that kept abandoning my own boundaries hoping love would eventually feel safe if I sacrificed enough.

Therapy forced me to confront the little girl inside me who learned very early that love often arrived attached to pain.

That little girl grew into a woman who tolerated emotional neglect, inconsistency, betrayal, chaos, and self-abandonment because some part of me still believed hurt was simply the price people paid to avoid being alone.

And once I finally saw that pattern clearly…

I could not unsee it anymore.

Meanwhile, my relationship with Alex continued shifting beneath the weight of reality too.

The same emotional intensity that initially felt intoxicating sometimes became overwhelming once survival mode slowed down enough for us both to breathe. We loved each other deeply, but we also triggered each other deeply.

That is the complicated truth about wounded people finding comfort in one another.

Sometimes love exists there.

But so do unresolved wounds.

And unresolved wounds eventually demand attention no matter how beautiful the connection feels initially.

For the first time in my life, I stopped asking:

"Who loves me?"

And started asking:

"Why do I keep equating chaos with love in the first place?"

That question changed everything.

Healing is not simply learning how to leave unhealthy situations.

Healing is learning why unhealthy situations felt emotionally familiar enough for me to stay inside them for so long.

And somewhere between therapy sessions, long nights alone, uncomfortable truths, and emotional unraveling...

I began meeting myself for the first time.

Not the wife.

Not the caretaker.

Not the woman performing strength.

Just me.

Stripped of titles.

Stripped of survival tactics.

Stripped of the versions of myself I created to make other people comfortable.

I was emotionally naked...

and trying to redress this new version of myself without reaching back for the pain that once clothed me.

And although that process was painful...

it was also the beginning of freedom in its truest form.

LEE

As time passed and the emotional smoke finally began clearing, I found myself thinking about my marriage differently.

Not with rage.

Not even with resentment.

Mostly with understanding.

That surprised me.

Because when relationships end painfully, people often want a villain. Someone to point at. Someone to blame completely so the ending feels easier to justify emotionally.

But the truth about Lee and me was far more complicated than that.

Our marriage was not built on hatred.

It was built on survival.

On youth.

On longing.

On two wounded people trying to love each other with emotional tools neither of us fully possessed yet.

For many years, we did the best we could.

That matters to me deeply now.

Because despite everything that happened between us, I never want to erase the love that existed simply because the relationship eventually stopped working.

Lee loved me the best way he knew how.

I believe that genuinely.

He protected.

Provided.

Sacrificed.

Worked hard.

Showed up.

And for the version of me that entered the marriage all those years ago, that kind of love felt like enough.

One thing I never questioned with Lee was whether he would physically protect me.

Never.

Standing six-foot-three and over three hundred pounds, his presence alone made most people think twice before approaching me disrespectfully. When I was with him, I moved through the world differently.

Safer.

More relaxed.

I never had to constantly scan rooms.

Never had to calculate danger the same way I did growing up.

Lee became my personal bodyguard in many ways.

And after a childhood where I rarely felt emotionally or physically safe, that kind of protection mattered more to me than I probably even understood at the time.

I did not realize how much I depended on that sense of security until it was gone.

One evening after our separation, Alex and I went to a local bar together.

At some point during the night, a man suddenly approached our table aggressively and asked:

"What are you looking at?"

To this day, I honestly do not even think I looked at him long enough to provoke anything.

But something about our presence offended him.

He stood directly in front of our table staring us down in a way that immediately shifted the energy around us.

The tension felt thick.

Unpredictable.

Dangerous.

Eventually, Alex and I left abruptly because the situation no longer felt safe.

And for the first time since leaving my marriage, I felt the full weight of what I no longer had access to emotionally.

I could not call Lee.

I no longer had the towering man whose mere presence made me feel protected in public spaces.

And suddenly, beneath all my growth, healing, and independence…

I felt like that scared little girl again.

The little girl who learned early that safety could disappear quickly.

That realization humbled me deeply because it forced me to confront something uncomfortable:

Even unhealthy relationships can still contain things we genuinely grieve losing.

And part of grieving my marriage meant grieving the safety I associated with him too.

At one point in my life, Lee was the center of my world.

Completely.

I built my identity around being his wife, building our family, supporting his career, protecting our home, and preserving the life we created together. I was comfortable making myself smaller inside the relationship because somewhere deep down, I believed sacrifice was proof of love.

He probably believed the same thing too.

That is why I no longer see either of us as entirely right or entirely wrong.

We were two people loving each other through the lens of our own wounds, conditioning, fears, and emotional limitations.

The hardest truth for me to accept was this:

Lee had not fundamentally changed over the years.

I had.

For a long time, the version of me that existed inside our marriage fit him perfectly. She tolerated more. Needed less. Centered everyone else before herself. Accepted emotional inconsistency as long as loyalty and provision remained intact.

But eventually, I outgrew her.

And once I started emotionally evolving, our relationship no longer fit the same way it once had.

That realization hurt both of us.

Because growth is beautiful...

but growth also disrupts every relationship built around older versions of yourself.

I understand now why the new version of me frightened him.

The woman I was becoming no longer revolved entirely around him emotionally. I started prioritizing my own voice, my own healing, my own creativity, my own desires, my own peace.

And after years of being the emotional center of my world, that shift probably felt like abandonment to him.

And I cannot fully blame him for struggling with it.

Because I struggled with it too.

There were moments during the collapse of our marriage where we both hurt each other deeply. Moments where pride, fear, resentment, jealousy, and emotional exhaustion brought out ugly parts of both of us.

And I have had to take accountability for my part in that too.

I allowed certain behaviors for years.

I normalized disrespect.

I performed acceptance in situations that hurt me emotionally because I was afraid confronting the truth would cost me my marriage.

In many ways, my silence taught him what I was willing to tolerate.

That does not excuse the pain we caused each other.

But accountability requires honesty.

And honesty means admitting I participated in dynamics that slowly destroyed parts of me too.

Still…

despite everything…

I do not regret my marriage.

That may confuse some people, but it is true.

My marriage gave me my children.

It gave me stability during seasons when I desperately needed it.

It taught me lessons about love, survival, sacrifice, identity, boundaries, and self-worth that I may never have learned otherwise.

My marriage served its purpose.

And I say that now not with bitterness…

but gratitude.

Because not every relationship is meant to last forever in order to matter deeply.

Some relationships exist to build you.

Some exist to break you open.

Some exist to mirror the wounds you still need to heal.

And some exist simply to walk with you through one season of your life before releasing you into the next.

Lee deserved someone who loved him without compromise.

And honestly…

so did I.

In the end, I did not leave because I hated him.

I left because I finally understood that love should not require abandoning myself to preserve it.

And once I learned that lesson, there was no returning to the woman I used to be.

REASON

For most of my life, I believed love required suffering.

Not consciously.

No one sat me down and taught me that lesson directly.

But life did.

My childhood did.

My relationships did.

The women before me did.

Somewhere along the way, I learned that love meant enduring. Sacrificing. Waiting. Shrinking. Forgiving endlessly. Carrying pain quietly so other people could remain comfortable.

And because of that, I spent years confusing survival with devotion.

If I stayed, I loved you.

If I tolerated it, I loved you.

If I broke myself trying to save the relationship, then surely that meant the love was real.

But healing forced me to confront a truth I spent most of my life avoiding:

Love should not require the slow destruction of yourself to sustain it.

That realization changed everything.

Not overnight.

Not dramatically.

Quietly.

Slowly.

Like sunlight creeping into a dark room after years of closed curtains.

For a long time, I blamed other people for my unhappiness.

Lee.

My childhood.

The women.

The chaos.

The emotional wounds.

And while many of those experiences genuinely hurt me, eventually I had to confront the harder truth too:

No one forced me to keep abandoning myself.

At some point, I became responsible for healing the parts of me that believed pain was normal.

That accountability changed my life.

Healing is not becoming perfect.

Healing is becoming aware.

Aware of my patterns.

Aware of my wounds.

Aware of the ways I betrayed myself hoping other people would finally choose me correctly.

And once awareness arrives, I could no longer pretend not to see the truth.

The truth was, I had spent years searching for love externally while neglecting the relationship I had with myself entirely.

I wanted people to choose me while I consistently abandoned myself.

I wanted emotional safety while ignoring my own boundaries.

I wanted peace while remaining emotionally attached to chaos because chaos felt familiar.

But eventually, exhaustion forces honesty.

And honesty forced me back to myself.

Not the wife.

Not the mother.

Not the woman trying desperately to keep everyone else emotionally comfortable.

Just Anise.

The little girl inside me who wanted love so badly she accepted almost any version of it offered to her.

The woman inside me who finally learned she deserved more than survival.

Healing did not magically erase my grief.

I still mourned my marriage.

Still mourned versions of myself.

Still mourned relationships that felt transformative even when they became painful.

But grief and gratitude can exist together.

That was another lesson healing taught me.

I can appreciate the people who helped shape me without needing to remain attached to every chapter they occupied.

And maybe that is what maturity truly is.

Not bitterness.

Not blame.

Not pretending I was innocent in every situation.

But understanding.

Compassion.

Accountability.

Release.

My decision to leave was never simply about heartbreak.

It was about legacy.

I needed my children to see that love should never cost them their identity.

I needed my children to understand that loving someone does not mean abandoning reason, self-respect, or peace to keep a relationship alive.

I needed them to know that choosing yourself is not selfish when staying requires your destruction.

Children do not only listen to what we say.

They absorb what we model.

And I refused to teach mine that suffering endlessly in the name of love was noble.

Today, when I think about the woman standing at that fork in the road between love and reason, I no longer see weakness.

I see a woman exhausted from carrying everyone else before finally learning how to carry herself.

I see a woman terrified to choose herself because she had been conditioned to believe choosing herself meant selfishness.

But it wasn't selfishness.

It was survival of a different kind.

The kind where I finally stopped abandoning myself to keep other people comfortable.

The kind where peace became more attractive than emotional chaos.

The kind where healing mattered more than being chosen.

And for the first time in my life, I finally understood this:

Some people enter your life forever.

Others enter to transform you.

And sometimes the greatest act of love is knowing when it is time to let go.

ACKNOWLEDGMENTS

To my cousin Nicole,

My unofficial and extremely unlicensed therapist.

Thank you for being the calm in every storm I created around myself. Thank you for always answering the phone, even when life was heavy for you too. You never told me what I wanted to hear. You told me what I needed to hear, even when the truth was uncomfortable, even when I was too stubborn, emotional, or hardheaded to fully receive it in the moment.

You listened without judgment.

You grounded me when my emotions were louder than my logic.

You reminded me who I was whenever I started losing myself inside pain, relationships, fear, or chaos.

So much of this healing journey was possible because I had someone willing to sit beside me honestly while I unraveled and rebuilt myself at the same time.

You have been more than family to me.

You have been my safe place.

My sounding board.

My protector.

My best friend.

And through every version of me, you always managed to see the woman underneath all the survival.

The real me.

FUCKING AMAZING.

I love you forever.
Thank you for seeing me.

Made in the USA
Coppell, TX
13 June 2026

81369572R00073